A Visit to
Grand Canyon
National Park

by Chris Martin

Table of Contents

Introduction

The Grand Canyon is a natural wonder of the world. It has mile-high walls and a raging, racing, rock-cutting river. And it's one of the greatest national parks in the United States or anywhere else.

The Grand Canyon is also a record of time, almost 2 billion years. The canyon tells a story about the earth in rock. In this tale, volcanoes, earthquakes, and long-ago oceans created rocks. Wind, rain, ice, and snow changed these rocks. Water sawed, sliced, and carved them to form the Grand Canyon. For all these reasons, Grand Canyon National Park is like no other place on Earth.

Fantastic Canyon	
Age of Oldest Rock in Grand Canyon	Almost 2 billion years old and counting
Length of Canyon	277 miles (436 kilometers)
Depth of Canyon	Average depth is 4,000 feet (1,219 meters) Deepest point is 6,000 feet (1,828 meters) (more than one mile!)
Width of Canyon	18 miles (28 kilometers) at its widest Just 100 feet (30 meters) at its narrowest
Size of Park	1,218,375 acres—bigger than the whole state of Rhode Island
Layers of Rock	Almost 40 layers of rock in the canyon walls
Hidden Secret	About 1,000 caves!

Chapter One

Taking It All In

Before you learn the story of the canyon, take a look at it. Your view begins at about 7,000 feet (2,133 meters). You are standing on top of a **plateau**, a large, high, flat land area.

Take that first look down. Far, far below, about one mile down, is a river that looks like a tiny, dark thread. It's the Colorado River. All around and above it are colorful and spectacular layers of rock.

The rock layers come in all colors. You can see orange, deep red, green, tan, gray, and even pink and purple layers. Rising at so many different angles and heights, the rocks appear steep, mysterious, and beautiful.

The view seems to go on forever. The canyon is 277 miles (445 kilometers) long and 18 miles (28 kilometers) across at its widest point. That is quite a view to take in at first glance!

Next, you are probably wondering what else this amazing place holds.

↻ Views of the Grand Canyon are guaranteed to be spectacular.

Locating the Grand Canyon

The Grand Canyon lies on the Colorado Plateau. It is in the southwestern United States in the state of Arizona.

Next, find the Colorado River, which begins far off this map in the Rocky Mountains. Start on the right side of the map to trace the river's course west through the park. After leaving the park, the Colorado River flows across the Mexican border and into the Gulf of California.

Cartographers:
We'd Be Lost Without Them

Cartographers are mapmakers. They study the surface of the earth. Much of their work involves measurements and calculations. They put the information they gather into forms that people can understand, usually maps. People use the maps to find their way around.

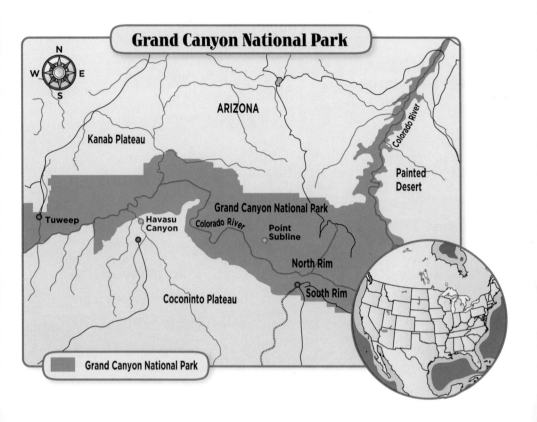

Now look at the map above to find the North Rim and the South Rim. The **rims** are the tops of the canyon. You'll learn more about them later. This map shows some of the most important **landforms** in the park, such as rivers, streams, mountains, and plateaus.

Chapter Two

Landforms and Climate

The park's many different bodies of water are important landforms. Of course, the Colorado River is the main river that flows through it, but the park also contains many major streams. The Little Colorado River is a major stream. Like many of the other streams, it feeds into the Colorado River. The river, streams, and springs create a water system in the park.

Most of these streams do not flow all year. In spring, the streams rush along, filled with melted snow. But in the hot summer months, they shrink to a trickle or even dry up.

Some of the streams ➲ form beautiful waterfalls as they flow down the steep sides of the canyon.

🎧 Why do you think a mesa is sometimes called a tableland?

As you begin to explore the Grand Canyon, you will see many other landforms, including mesas and buttes. A **mesa** is a flat-topped mountain, like a plateau but smaller. A **butte** is a flat-topped high hill or ridge with steep sides that is smaller than a mesa. Take a moment to admire how the different heights and angles of the various landforms give the park its striking beauty.

Geologists:
Their Job Rocks

Geologists study how the earth formed and how it changes. They study rocks, mountains, oceans, volcanoes, and other parts of the planet. They often supervise exploring for sources of energy, such as oil. They look for metals we need, like copper. They also help us understand and prepare for earthquakes.

⌂ Winter can bring more than 100 inches of snow to the North Rim.

⌂ Summer is a time for thunderstorms on the South Rim.

⌂ The inner canyon is hot and dry. Near the river, summer temperatures often soar above 100°F (38°C).

Climate

In the summer most of the land in the Grand Canyon is dry and dusty. But the climate does vary from place to place. On the North Rim, which is higher than the South Rim, the climate is cooler, rainier, and snowier than in other areas of the park. On the drier South Rim, rainfall is lower than on the North Rim. You'll see fewer trees, too.

People who make the trip down into the canyon itself must get ready to be very hot. If they stay overnight, they must be prepared for the cold. The canyon's desert climate means hot days and cold nights.

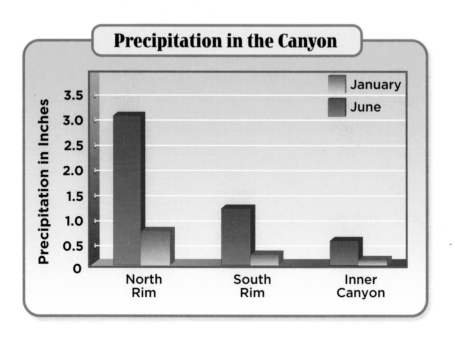

Chapter Three

How the Canyon Formed

Can you guess what main force created the Grand Canyon? It was the mighty Colorado River.

The Colorado is a huge, powerful river. In the spring melted snow fills the river and it becomes swift and wild. The river picks up rocks, huge boulders, sand, and pebbles and carries them along. Over millions of years, this gritty river water carved into layer after layer of rock. It carved the deepest canyon of all, the Grand Canyon.

Layers of Rock

One reason the river could carve the rock is that the rock was soft. Soft for rock, that is! Back in time, before there was a Grand Canyon, oceans covered the land.

Over millions of years, broken seashells, sand, mud, and clay fell to the bottom of the sea.

These small bits of matter that settle on the sea bottom are called **sediment**. Over millions of years, the sediment turned into rock, called **sedimentary rock**. And this rock was soft enough for the river to be able to carve a deeper and deeper path through it.

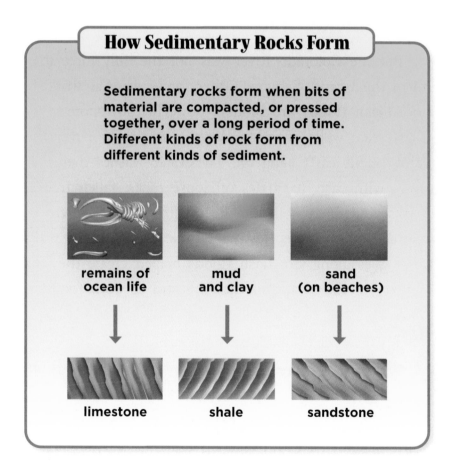

How Sedimentary Rocks Form

Sedimentary rocks form when bits of material are compacted, or pressed together, over a long period of time. Different kinds of rock form from different kinds of sediment.

remains of ocean life

mud and clay

sand (on beaches)

limestone

shale

sandstone

Fast-flowing Water

But the Colorado River was not the only force to form the Grand Canyon. Other forces were at work, too. **Flash floods** are sudden, powerful downpours that create walls of water. When water rushes over the land, plants can't hang on. The water washes them away with ease. It carries off loose rocks, fallen trees, sticks, and dusty soil, too. Everything washes down the canyon in a fast-flowing bundle, carving new walls as it goes along. So, flash floods helped create the canyon in the past, and they are still at work today.

Ice

Water helped create the canyon in another way. It seeped into small cracks between the rocks and then froze. The ice expanded, making the cracks bigger, until pieces of rocks broke off and crashed down into the canyon. The freezing and melting of water is still carving the canyon today.

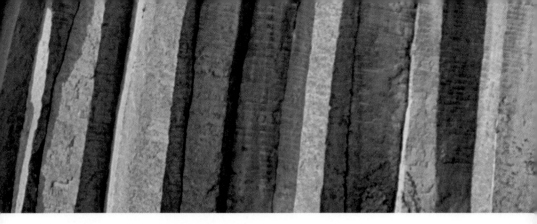

⌒ Basalt forms from liquid rock called lava.

Volcanoes and Earthquakes

Another force at work on the canyon was hot rock—really hot rock from volcanoes, that is. It flowed out of the ground to dam the canyon many times. Once cool, it formed a hard rock called **basalt**. You can see it on some of the walls of the canyon. Also, while the canyon formed, earthquakes pushed the land up. The canyon got deeper and higher.

Layers of Past Life

The story of life in the canyon is fused into its rocks. **Fossils**, the remains of plants or animals that lived long ago, tell this life story. Imagine that you are hiking up from the bottom of the canyon. In the lowest layers of the canyon walls are the oldest fossils in the park. They are of one-celled animals.

⋒ Each layer in the Grand Canyon tells a story.

Paleontologists:
They Dig Their Work

Paleontologists
are fossil hunters.
They search for and
identify the remains
of long-ago life.
Some paleontologists
look for the remains
of dinosaurs. But
dinosaurs are just
one tiny part of the
whole fossil record.
There are many other
fascinating things to
find, including the
remains of life in
ancient seas.

In the middle layers, the fossils are about 400 million years old. These fossils are of fish, insects, and plants. Near the top of the canyon are fossils of more recent animals from the age of dinosaurs. Because the fossils go up the canyon from oldest to youngest, the Grand Canyon has been called a "ladder of life."

People search   ⮑
for fossils in the
Grand Canyon.

Chapter Four

Fun in the Canyon

Now that you've learned how the Grand Canyon was formed, it's time to pay it a serious visit. Most people drive, ride in tour buses, or take the national park shuttle buses along the South Rim. But your conscience is telling you that the best way to see the park is from inside the canyon.

For a great experience, lace up those hiking boots. You don't have to go far, and you don't have to have great physical coordination. If you're a frustrated photographer, now's your chance.

◑ Don't just sit in a car! Take an active look.

If you're in good shape, you might decide to hike all the way to the bottom of the canyon. You'll need real hiking boots. And you'll need to bring plenty of water.

This hike will take you all day. Start early in the morning when it is cooler. Rest in the heat of the day. And return well before dark.

Saddle Up?

Does a mule ride sound great? Well, hold your horses for a minute. You need to:

- be at least 4 feet 7 inches tall.

- weigh less than 200 pounds (you WILL be weighed).

- be in good shape.

Some people explore the canyon from the back of a mule! These trips are long and hot, and they are not easy. But many people call them the best ride of their life.

↻ A mule ride to the bottom of the canyon takes about five hours.

18

⌒ For excitement, nothing beats a river rafting trip.

Run the Rapids

If hiking or riding a mule are not exciting enough for you, how about riding the rapids! You do this on a raft. These trips are long—from three days to three weeks. But you'll see the scenery of a lifetime. Sometimes you'll slide calmly through the canyon. Other times you'll hang on tight as your raft leaps and lurches through crashing water. Talk about thrills and chills!

↷ Going backcountry can be the best way to get away from it all!

Camping

With so many exciting things to do in the Grand Canyon, you might want to stay longer. Would you like to wake up to the smell of fresh pine? Then camping might be the best way for you to stay. The Grand Canyon has campsites that are open all year long.

If you're willing to hike, you can try a true wilderness experience called backcountry. Going backcountry means hiking past the crowds and daytrippers. You load up a pack with supplies and prepare to sleep out on your own.

Conclusion

You've seen what an amazing place the Grand Canyon is. And you've learned how its walls tell the story of what happened on Earth over millions of years.

Someday maybe you can visit the Grand Canyon in person. If you do, hike in. Ride the rapids. Read the story the rocks tell you. Feel the layers of rock change under your hand from chalky to hard and grainy to smooth. And have a rockin' good time!

Leave it as it is; you cannot improve on it; not a bit.

— President Theodore Roosevelt about the Grand Canyon

Glossary

basalt *(buh-SAWLT)* hard rock that is formed when lava cools *(page 15)*

butte *(BEWT)* a high hill or ridge with a flat top and steep sides; a butte is smaller than a mesa *(page 9)*

cartographer *(kahr-TAWG-ruh-fur)* a mapmaker *(page 6)*

flash flood *(FLASH FLUD)* a sudden rushing wall of water. Flash floods helped form the canyon. *(page 14)*

fossil *(FOS-uhl)* The remains of plants and animals that lived long ago *(page 15)*

geologist *(jee-OL-uh-jist)* a person who studies Earth and how it changes *(page 9)*

landform *(LAND-fawrm)* a feature on Earth's surface like a mountain, valley, or plateau *(page 7)*

mesa *(MAY-suh)* a hill or mountain with a flat top and steep sides; like a plateau but smaller *(page 9)*

paleontologist *(pay-lee-uhn-TOL-uh-jist)* a person who searches for and identifies the remains of long-ago life *(page 16)*

plateau *(pla-TOH)* a very large area of flat land that rises steeply above the surrounding land *(page 4)*

rim *(RIM)* the outer edge *(page 7)*

sediment *(SED-uh-muhnt)* sand, broken bits of shell, and other materials that form layers and can turn to rock *(page 13)*

sedimentary rock *(sed-uh-MEN-tuh-ree ROK)* Rock that is formed from sediments. Examples of sedimentary rocks include limestone, sandstone, and shale. *(page 13)*

Index

Comprehension Check

Summarize

Look back at this book. What do you think is the most important idea in each chapter? Use the Judgment Chart to help you summarize the four chapters to tell what you learned about the Grand Canyon.

Action ➜ Judgment
➜
➜
➜
➜

Think About It

1. The author says the Grand Canyon is like no other place on Earth. Do you agree? List three facts from this book that help you make your judgment. *(Make Judgments)*

2. In the last chapter, the author describes different ways to see the canyon. Which type of trip would you like best? Which type of trip would you like least? Explain your answer. *(Analyze)*

3. More visitors go to the Grand Canyon every year. This results in pollution and crowding in some areas. Should the number of visitors to the park be limited, or should everyone have the chance to see this wonderful canyon at any time? Explain your answer. *(Apply/Evaluate)*